Holding Ground

Holding Ground

Bruce Willard

Four Way Books
Tribeca

for my family, always,
everywhere you are

Please direct all inquiries to:
Editorial Office
Four Way Books
POB 535, Village Station
New York, NY 10014
www.fourwaybooks.com

Library of Congress Cataloging-in-Publication Data

Willard, Bruce.
  Holding ground / Bruce Willard.
      p. cm.
  Includes bibliographical references.
  Poems.
  ISBN 978-1-935536-28-4 (pbk. : alk. paper)
  I. Title.
  PS3623.I5534H65 2013
  811'.6--dc23

                          2012029326

This book is manufactured in the United States of America
and printed on acid-free paper.

Four Way Books is a not-for-profit literary press. We are grateful for the assistance
we receive from individual donors, public arts agencies, and private foundations.

State of the Arts

NYSCA

This publication is made possible with public funds
from the New York State Council on the Arts, a state agency.

[clmp]   We are a proud member
         of the Council of Literary Magazines and Presses.

Distributed by University Press of New England
One Court Street, Lebanon, NH 03766

CONTENTS

"there's a flame in me that thinks
and a wind for fire and for sails"
—Zbigniew Herbert

I.

WHAT I WANT

I want to be heard, not seen,
the voice late night on FM between sets,
the blues which sounds hollow and full,
a fog horn in the fog at noon.

I want to be read slowly, out loud,
heard like wind, close, but from some distance.

A footfall which says, I'm coming *to an uncarpeted hall,*
a word which says, I'm here *to the dark.*

GOOD MORNING

I am greeting this life
I have awakened to,
the clothes I've slept in
still warm on my back,
blood-orange sun on the wall
next to the bed, regular sound
of traffic on the street,
like there was no more
pressing purpose than to rise
fully dressed, hand-part my hair
and meet the day
wearing the layers I've lived in
all these hours.

DOPPLER

I need the promise of weather-
radar, frontal times, the vagaries
of course. Animated,

blooming cells spinning counter-
clockwise; ridges of pressure
advancing, accordioning

over state lines to the west.
I need the promise of maximum
and minimum—wind, temperature,

seductions of moisture—dew point,
wind chill, humidity. I want
my conditions relatively—one-part

density and reflection, another
anticipation and weathering resolve.

BIRD CALL

Daybreak greedy but weak.
The snowplow's blue light
rounding the room.

A magpie squawks.
I wish you no hope, it says.
Blessing from the kingdom of long odds.

BETWEEN

Thirty-two years between
Rockies and the Pacific, Kolob and the coast.
Between Damariscotta and Boothbay,
cypress and sugar maple, jacaranda
and aspen. Between opening
and closing. Between time zones, climates,
license plates, telephone numbers.
Laundry mixed with luggage,
keys to locks long gone.

Night blows between the frames of houses,
winding, unwinding clotheslines, between
pant legs, between sleeves, between selves.

EKG

On thermal tape, subaudible,
the thump-pulse of bass,
as from a passing car. Afterwards,

the regular sound of water
in a fountain and wind
in the leathery leaves of sycamore.

My heart surrounded
in its cage of branches—
sentry quail, whippoorwill scout—
calling, waiting, calling
for some relative, kindred
sound to call its own.

FAMILY PORTRAIT

I was close to my brother
but not as close as I wanted to be.
The light was warm, diffused.
The color of a bruise
as it starts to fade. My parents
were there and my grandmother
in a yard at the beginning
of a home that's now gone.

What time of the day was it?

I wanted my brother in the center.
I wanted the sun
to graze his slender legs, his discolored
biceps. I wanted to see
him as I saw myself.

Who took the shot?

Everyone was talking. I could not see
the camera, the way it moved
angle to angle to conceal
the space between us.

How much older are you than him?

It was late in the day. The sun
strained to measure the years

between us. Everyone
was talking, one over another,
their voices like the layers of emulsion
on a photograph.

Did it take long?

I stood behind my brother. I could feel
his buzz cut hair under my chin,
his nervous elbows against my chest.
I imagined a perfect photo,
the story it would tell.

How long did it take?

The light was failing.
There was a sudden flash.
The camera's clunking sound—
a coin being dropped
into a china bank full of coins.
I was struck by the darkness
inside the bank, the shiny enamel
outside. How it would break
if I tried to get the coins out.
It took forever.

II.

JOY IS SORROW UNMASKED

The blues reopens every room
I enter; a smell
I have been preparing to miss.

A day is a ballad;
play it round and slow. The refrain
returns; the melody goes.

A dream is a woman;
play it sweet and low.
Every tender has its touch.

INTIMATE

All day I have been trying to say something
about something without talking
about the thing itself.

Here's a bed of fresh-cut, green grass,
here's a blanket of warm sunlight,
here's my sound; mouth it gently. Please

don't forget me.

WORDS

I'm putting up soup today
the way I put up firewood:
my desk stacked with cords
of carrots; broccoli, limbed
and green; billets of meat
for toothy flavor; potatoes
for slow heat. Two knotty,
sweet, red peppers. Parsley,
mint, and lemon grass, of course.

When the fire's kindled,
when the souping begins,
I stir to the point
sweet becomes savory-sour.
Where the garlic of ash
meets the cilantro of *albóndigas*.

For the place taste insists,
turns back on itself,
syllables smoking, flames
banking against the cool
grate of night.

NOTHING BECOMES ME

I call frequently
but talk less each month

sometimes I try
to get off the phone

as soon as it is answered
before the conversation turns

the way this poem is turning now

think comma
when you think of me

listen
for the space between

my lips
too lean for words

HURRICANE WATCH

end of summer
last day of the month

persimmon maple
sunflower birch
burnt oak   flagging
in their districts   indolent

air syrupy
and warm leaves

gale warning
in effect   and rain
heavy at times

.

III.

SO WHAT

if the timing isn't as expected
if the flowers surge
after the leaves begin to blow

so what
if the piano and horns come in
behind the snap of the bass

so what
if the sun rises late
from its home of hills

there is more
than enough space
between the clouds

more
to the rest of the song
sparrow's song

than the trill,
two-note question it plies
one hundred ways:

so what
so what is there
to say?

AUGUST

Fall is in the air, she said.
But the day looked no different
than a day in June,

no different than the way change
opens the blank book of your hands.

To the south a hurricane was forming,
words gathering, moisture gaining,

winds circling the blind,
dry eye of summer.

DEW POINT

Through glass he watched shampoo
stream and braid, drain the creek bed
of her back. Stratus steam gathering
'round her knees.

When the first drops bloomed on the glass,
a certain density was reached.
Water pooled, gathering momentum.
He felt its gravity,

his thirst searching for seams in stone.

ISLAND

You can talk to me now, she said.
The windows were open and I heard
the whine of traffic stop and the clang
of a bell which meant a bridge was closing.
I heard a train heading south,
the sound of ferries leaving the pier.

Don't you have anything you want to say? she asked.
When I looked out the window
I saw stars through a thin layer of clouds
and the night which shows and covers
the faint pulse of airplanes miles from Earth.

I could not remember the name of a single island
the ferries cross between.

IN OTHER WORDS

It was late and we finished
each other's sentences
the way couples do when they know
a story but dislike its ending.

Canyon winds pushed against the house,
branches scraped the shingles,
peeled back flashing. We listened
for breaks in the words.

I said, *People do not say what they mean*
in order to keep their story alive.
It was fall and the ground was clear
of must. Clean of the blood

of chlorophyll. You asked, *Why*
did you fall in love with me? I said
that I felt sorry for you. *Why*
did you fall in love with me? you asked.

I spoke but the wind took my words.

HOLDING GROUND

Let's look for shelter, he said.
Fog dulled his words, made everything
far away sound near. Each and every
obstacle. Like the waves on passing ledges.

If you keep watch to port,
I'll watch to starboard, he offered.
Water gathered on both sides of the cabin
windows. Water matted her hair. Water drowned
the air between east and west.

There's an island with a cove at the north end
and good holding ground inside, he said.
The current at the mouth of the river bent
over markers and buoys giving the illusion
of speed over ground.

Release the hook, he called.
The windlass played out chain and the anchor
found bottom. He could not see the bow
from the helm. They could no longer
see each other.

We must watch for drift, he said.
Or thought. When an hour went by
without drag, *Home,* he whispered.
Yes, she said, descending below
where water insulates as it steals warmth,
deafens as it covers ground.

THE CAT

He listened to her speak the whole drive home.
Sudden, dark words that move
cumulatively, by degrees.
When she was finished, the way seemed clear

of choices. From eye's edge, a cat darted.
There was an almost imperceptible
bump and a shadow shimmied across the lane.
He pulled over the truck. Left it running.

In the brush, the cat lay stretched out.
Hissed as he approached,
dragged its rear legs. Then again.

On the ground, he found a branch like a divining
stick, one end a "Y," the other a slender tail.
Listening for life as one listens for water,
he placed the open end on the animal's neck.

Waited. And again.
And pushed. And pushed
until the flat hiss of silence
closed in on the night,

the sound of the truck idling
in the darkness, the road ahead.

DIVORCE

There was a dry, simple thinness
to the air. An archipelago
made off to the south—
the debris of continental drift.

Everything was said
in three or four ways.
Every goddamned thing done.

Just the word remained. Like an island
the morning after a cold front had passed.

THE RHYTHM METHOD

When he went to bed he wondered
how sleep would come;
how would he know it,
where it would take him?
Would he hear trees
and steady rain? How long
would his ankles circle
the comfort of small repetitions?

When he went to bed
he felt wasted by his desires.
Not because they were large
but because they were so hungry;
ravenous, you could say.
A withering in his abdomen.

When he went to bed
he felt a little of himself
dying. More than the normal
amount, more than the usual
ache. Waves of darkness
advancing and retreating,
but never making ground.

IV.

PRAYER

Lord, give me what you've already given
Until I unbelieve it so thoroughly
I believe again.

The winter is untrue;
The blessed wind repeats, repeats.
Snow buries and reburies the earth. Still,

The earth reappears.
How do I come to know anything?
Where, in an instant, I know years

Through the hand of my child
And grow not to know the parents
I've held and become?

Soon I will become unknowable—
To my children, to my wife,
To the snow. Wind, uncover me.

Release the music and the nose:
The foot-tap which outlives silence,
The bare earth which loosens to give up its smell.

PERENNIAL

I was tired of wanting,
tired of morning,
tired of the way the ocean waits
for the sun to set.

I was tired of thawing,
tired of spring.
Tired of hoping
bulbs would rise

and when they did,
I was tired of the longing,
sexual smell of the earth,
so expectedly ugly,
so eager,

there was nothing
left to want.

PLAN B

The heater blows air but no warmth.
The phone will not connect.
The washing machine turns over
the same soiled suds.
Windows let in the thief of night.

After dark, the power fails.
When it returns, electricity
floods the pride of candles.

Look at me.
I'll love you forever,
promises Power.

Go, repair to the night,
says the dark.

THE THINGS I COLLECTED

I collected mussel shells
turning indigo to lilac.
Then pinecones, toothy and long.
And rocks from beaches and alongside
streams, smooth and oval as an eyelid,
striped across, waiting to open.

There were acorns, driftwood, leaves,
buoys, and glass of every color.
But especially the colors
of the day—the marginal
light of dawn, warm and pale,
the fever of sunset, transparent,
blood-red on the backs of my eyelids.

PARLOR

A month before summer, I woke
to a dream of rising
in the still humid night,
setting out from the co-op before dawn
to the grounds between two rivers.

With the first haul of traps, I drew remnants
of sunken objects—ironware pots
and Mason jars. The second string
brought doubloons of gold.
With the third string, osprey and loon flew
from the parlor of each trap.

I wanted to tell you everything
but I fell back asleep. When I woke,
I motored to the grounds
between two rivers,

hauled in a record catch.
In the evening you celebrated me listening
to the warblings of the loon at dusk,
thinking of the night ahead—the way it gives
openly to the coming day
and to haulings from the deep.

GREAT PLAINS

I could drive for days without fear
of outrunning these patchwork clouds,

bridge lines of cumulus
this way or that towards the horizon,

midway between one place
and another, standing up
to the administrations of wind.

I like a destination which pulls
true, deliberate,
but at great distance. Like

I like the slow, imperceptible
progress of knowing
but not knowing
how far I'll travel today,
where I'll find gas
for the next leg
or when.

SHE DIDN'T SAY A WORD

Her voice, a river
that overflows its sand banks, comes

with the stealth force of one
dozen tributaries

which rise in their balsam beds,
straightening the grass in bends,

leaving the alluvial slick
residue; her detritus

husked breathing
as passing benediction.

Night, when the rain comes
she returns—

all roads but one, downriver,
impassable. The narrow, wood

bridge over her consumed,
the island of me

surrounded, breathless, open-
mouthed.

CHEST TUBE

I breached like a refrigerator door
being parted. Suction and abundance.
Vacuum and purge. A pond
swallowing a skipped stone.
A bag of chips exhaling at altitude.

I became audience to my emptying:
the colors—old ivy, whiskey, butterscotch,
gooseberry, oxblood. Then nothing
but hydrated air. An empty room.
Urgent in its equilibrium.

After the storm, the cottonwoods
were still, green. Me under their limbs, you
bent over me, lips full.
The tails of your words
upon my face. The suck of your kiss.
Everywhere the sound of air.

ASTRONOMY

The day the sculpture was completed,
you led me to a table of campers' projects,

yours beautiful in its simplicity—two bodies,
no galaxies or black holes.

You described the anatomy of eclipse,
the way the moon spins around the Earth,

or the other way around, orbit:
the frequency of an object's return.

I became part-time father that summer.
Week on, week off, the sun rose

in the afternoon at pick-up time.
In the morning the fog returned thick, obscuring

the circle of arm's reach. More than ten years
the marine layer has ghosted us.

We've traded positions. You, gaining speed
with distance. Me, finding weight

in the shadow of your passing.

FEBRUARY

My young daughter garnishes valentines
with hearts and cursive
words of equal size. Stands
them upright as hymnals
in the order of her affections:
Isaiah in front, then Ben, Miles, and Jake,
the girls respectfully behind.

Has anyone asked you
to be their valentine? I ask.
She drops her chin
and lifts her eyes
in quiet song. When I ask
if she will be mine,
her demur comes as thin refrain.

A section of green lawn breaks out
from the fence-line drift of snow
under a bold and cumulus sky.

FAMILIAR STORY

After the cottage was opened,
after the musty layers of winter were released,
after the flag was raised,
first for memory and then independence,
we never thought of home.

Not until August—the last week
of camp, the forwarding cards
mailed, the final lobsterbake,
moon and night hand in hand—
could the weight of raspberries be seen
glowing, fever red, pulling down the bushes.

Not until the thought of shuttering
did home become ready for putting up,
the flag of labor ready to fly.

MEN

We came to love women
The way we love a sense of place.
Through absence and smell.
Nose and dream.

We came to love women
The way we love our homes.
The leaving and loss.
The separation room from room.

We came to love women
The way we love our selves.
From a distance.
Loving what we long for most.

And then we didn't
Long, exactly, but for the silk
Of jasmine or tannin
Of spruce or cashmere.

Things we long to touch
And breathe
When we are far away.

GIVE AND TAKE

In Rangiroa, on the balcony of our *fare*,
I was fading like the moon, thinning

like the call of the frigate bird
in the palms

when you took me
in, behind you, at the railing,

and I gave long
and unexpectedly

because of your giving—
our mouths taking in

the molten air, our ears
taking in the wind,

the tide taking in
sand, giving back

waves, sandbars
before darkened water.

FOR SALE

Our house appeared in this morning's paper
and for a moment I forgot
whether we were buying or selling.
For a moment it seemed a place
with the right combination of rooms,
a view of the sea to the south,
and the mountains behind.

You would have thought we never lived here:
mornings with the kids before school,
the harmony of showers in the hall,
the nights we'd pass through pockets of warm and cold
on the way to the bedroom.
And you'd be right—home borrowed

as we borrow other things we call our own:
each other's breath when we make love,
our children's discoveries,
possessions we long for
when we've traded comfort
for the refuge of view,
sale for the refuge of something sold.

ARC

A barn owl calls from the oaks.
And there are others. Pairs
separated by night.
The dog across the street
barks, and in a lot across
town, another returns the call.
It is still night.

A deer turns its ear
to one across the road. A loon
gives its throat to shadow.
The dark is even.

Even night makes its chilled, flat
sound to the sky.
I am calling to you.
There is somewhere
to go. The air is teeming
with rain. Please.

V.

SAX

Reed to the wind
a throaty sound appears.
Weather across wood.

Feather upon flesh. Breath
over object. Not
me against me.

The wind blows three-quarters
time, one note for past, one present,
and one for rhythm.

Ballad of counter-
point, waltz of fire,
blue riff of bent air.

When the wind backs to the west,
my voicing comes modal,
smooth. Not brass, string, or reed.

Braid of joined breath,
response behind call, rest
inside each warming bar of air.

GOOD WORK

All day I have worked to earn the rain
that falls tonight from its purse
of clouds above this house.

Inside, full-round logs
on the fire, *Sketches of Spain*
on the radio, smell of love
in the covers, my children
all home from the storm.

So with the gutters talking
unanticipated accumulation,
I will spend the night fully
so that the trickle of small change
is the only runoff that gets away.

THE MARRIAGE

It wasn't happiness exactly. More
the way fields turn

late in the day
when sun is both contrast and color.

More the bent silence
syncopation loans to the blues.

More *been there* than *done that*—
a place returned to time

and again
despite the fog and traffic.

It was like perfection,
wind from the north,

a song sung
and loved once

more.

REVISED DIRECTIONS

Kids are pulling up road signs
so the easy landmarks—bump, sharp curve,
hidden drive—are gone.
If you're handy with an odometer and can subtract
where you've been from what you want,
you can still make it—
past the boatyard, before the church
converted to an art studio,
near the turnout along the creek
where the water pools up and sheets
over smooth ledge.

Look for the cutoff to the quarry
where girls are skinny-dipping
in the shimmering heat.
Where two or three boys watch,
a six-pack of "teeners" close
between them, cold malt
effervescent, unpredictable
in their throats.

PASSAGE

The rapid is runnable by day—
a tongue passing over a body
which bucks and rolls—
but I take to her at night
when she is nothing

but sound. Where the current quickens,
wind streams upriver, pushes my canoe
left and right, accelerates,
takes me in. Irredeemable,

I enter her, standing wave on wave,
souse hole, widow maker, keeper,
and eddy. In the after-water
her voice surrounds me. The current
makes song of the night.

BALSAMIC

I want to say everything
I know about intimacy

I know from doing.
My default desire

more telling
than my deficit gift of gab.

I want to say I'm more
show than tell,

better playing doctor
than playing:

a patient of my own
making. Impatient, hypocritical;

this itself
a loss for words.

Yesterday, I made balsamic dressing—
four sour, aged pints,

stirred to sweet, savory resolve,
the way a man is reduced, stirred

to action by an unspeakable thinness
in the morning air. His words, less

each year. More
acronyms, abbreviations:

skeleton words, boney
lines of text which say,

I'm here
but not here,

the way a double negative
is neither

positive nor negative
but something other.

ELEGY FOR THE STEPFATHER

Only a month ago I imagined sailing with him
on the ketch he built. His oversized hands
on the tiller. Sails fathered by a sou'west breeze.

He, who came like a front into my home
and stole my wind a decade ago.
Who gave it back in the way he tendered my son.
Trimmed the parts that were neither his nor mine
alone to love.

This strange, familial wind we rode and shared,
separated us, paired us on tack,
only to separate us again.

Becalmed, I miss him now,
just the small boat of his ashes left.
These storms which have no names,
the ghostly calm
which leaves no wake.

TIDES

There was week on and week off
and everything followed that cycle.

Trips to the grocery store to fill the "fridge,"
the changing of bedclothes, heating of bedrooms.

By mid-morning of the first day of weeks on
he counted the number of traps left to haul,

put aside objects they might share: a storm-
washed bottle, a sailor's log, the foyer of a trap.

The children knew the weeks
by the things they carried home

to home—essential, given things
swept to shore like a favorite cap

lost to the wind, returned to the sea.
He learned the weeks on like tides,

anticipating the height of water,
the way it covers obstacles, provides freeboard.

How weeks are short as days—
unable to contain full cycles of tide.

How the tide overflows, floods
the hours which shape it, floods

the week which drains away.

DOUBT

How I learned to catch
I can't be sure
though surely he taught me

the way you keep an eye
on the thing
which is strange

because that was all he had,
his other lost at war,
him thirty-four, me four;

both of us learning to see
meant judging the foreground
and background of a thing

to see the thing itself.
I doubt it worked
for me. I caught only colds

and once, years later, a girl
I did not deserve
who passed through my hands

the way something chronic
passes through
every happy day.

But he taught me doubt
joins us to what we want
to see: me how

I need to be seen,
him the double sense
he needs to see

safe passage
through a field
of charging men.

I doubt I said the word
back then, let alone observed,
at the center,

the silent "b,"
which shrinks beyond a shadow
of itself,

or the way a self-made man is made
from a deficit of self
and how, as father

to my own, I think
doubt is passed
with love

and love with doubt,
perhaps, though not as lasting
as the love which

passes back
and forth between us
while still it can.

VESSEL

This time they're snorkeling,
father and daughter,
and the water of the lagoon is still
enough to see the edges
of the reef beneath their boat,
the shouldering channels
through which the aqua blood
of the sea comes to them.

This time they're swimming
against the current that holds them
back, the surge of swells
that passes through heads of rock.
She's diving; she's found a treasure.
When she surfaces, she shows him.
He removes his mask, nods.

And it is as if the moment
connects every other moment
they know. Is a vessel
as the lagoon is a vessel
for the atoll,
its volcanic frame and bones more visible,
and the atoll is a vessel
for the sea to be held and be known.

Now they are sitting in their *fare*.
Ceiling fan dividing, re-dividing the day.
She hands him a ribboned basket;
he unwraps the packet, lifts a shell to the sky.
Voluminous, luminescent; a cloud blooming;
an atoll at the center of a shouldering sea.

THE AFTER LIFE

Son, once you stopped coming home
I could not stop missing you.
Now what I miss is more:
your bed so perfectly made
it withholds another life,
your shoes still
under its frame of sky,
your bureau drawers sticky
with the weather of closure.

Once I asked
how could I miss you
who I never knew
I wanted. Who,
years on, I needed
to know of whom
you were made. My
rogue wanting? Your
mother's flesh? Her
so long ago I cannot remember
what there is to miss.

And so I asked, was it me
I missed? Or more
the missing?
Columns of dust drafting
an old room
before windows of passing light.

After you were born
your afterbirth revealed two lives.
Once I thought I would have the other
if I could not have you.
I was the other.
How do I love the life
that's missing.

EVENING IN PAREA

The walkway lamps
have small geckos,
translucent
but for their eyes.
*I have nothing
but my hunger,*
they seem to say.

*I would not blink
at the rap and hum
of small insects.
I would not trade a tail
for stars.*

THRESHOLD

When he wakes his knees hurt.
And the soles of his feet.
I can feel all the miles I've walked, he says.

It feels like I've been with you each mile,
she replies. *My lower back is stiff.*
And this neck, it hurts any way I turn.

When he wakes he sits on the edge of the bed,
slides his hand under the covers and into the small
of her back. Round the jambs of her hips
to the tender joints which hinge
one to another.

She brings his knees to her,
framing her torso, working them
rhythmically, kneading
the ligaments, wanting
the tendons, drawing
the swollen muscles
across the threshold
that joins them.

Briefly, a door opens
as at the end of a long hall
that's suddenly shorter
and each buries
him or herself in the other, taking
leave of the night, making

the other their own, imagining
how he might succeed
her or she might succeed
him. Until they succeed each
other. Their coming
and going. The draft
which encircles them,
a corridor of light.

THE VIEW

In time
he saw how place becomes everything:
nights he'd listen to music
waking with the lights of town below,
walks to the coffee shop,
the widening space between
him and the leaves.

In time
he remembered how it'd be gone.
Not gone, but once removed,
less and less legible.
Something seen in abstract.
Leaves whose color displaces life
and fade.

Over time
the things he thought about became
as late afternoon sun on upholstery.
And he became the things he loved—
a small village once visited
whose narrow streets lead
to a port at the head of a broad bay
where the view becomes the place.

COUPLE

You said I was the gas
and someone needed to be
the brake. We never talked
of steering, choosing
the road. I guess
we always knew
which road we were on.

You said I was the gas
and someone needed to be
the brake. But we broke
so memorably,
broke with a flair
that kept us intact

barely aware of the winding
rush of air through our hair.
We were road-bound, driven,
between the shoulders, our hearts

moved by something we knew
not to name.

AUTOGRAPH

I held in script the shape of jazz—
"Johnny's Jeep," "Cootie's Concert,"
Ben's bridge to "Black, Brown and Beige."
I held in a signature
Duke's fingerprint whorl of sound,
the minor in each major
loop, the augmented seventh,
the proud, diminished root.
Each cursive letter arranged,
bent blue, blown to linear thinness.

In clouds, I saw the signature of sky;
in wind, the mark of the skin
touched and touching. Absence
in the sentimental, pairing
in the solos of the heart.

NOTES

"Joy Is Sorrow Unmasked" is the title of a song composed by Roy Hargrove from his album, *Earfood* (EmArcy, 2008).

"Elegy for the Stepfather" was written for Frank Louda (1947-2008), my son's stepfather.

"Doubt" is for my father.

"Vessel" is for my daughter, Savanna.

ACKNOWLEDGMENTS

Grateful acknowledgment is made to the editors of the following publications in which a number of these poems—some now in revised versions—first appeared:

5 A.M., *African American Review*, *AGNI Online*, *Connotation Press: An Online Artifact*, *Harvard Review*, *Mead Magazine*, and *Salamander*.

I also want to express my sincerest thanks to Ed Ochester, Susan Kinsolving, Major Jackson, and Sven Birkerts for their wisdom, inspiration, and guidance.

A big, heartfelt thanks also to Laure-Anne Bosselaar and Kurt Brown for their reading, invaluable advice and friendship, and to Martha Rhodes for her ear and generous flow of provocative suggestions.

Thank you to Liv, Sierra, Savanna, Glenn, and my parents for their support and endurance and to my wife, Jodie, for her patience and love.

Bruce Willard lives in California and Maine. An ex-disc jockey and forklift operator, he currently oversees several clothing catalog businesses and chauffeurs the family dogs from coast to coast each summer.